Hugs

For Your Heart

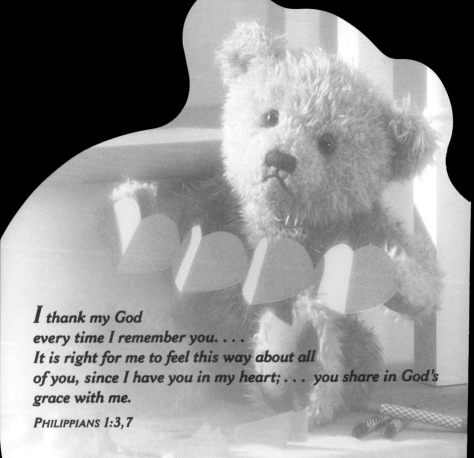

I thank my God
every time I remember you. . . .
It is right for me to feel this way about all
of you, since I have you in my heart; . . . you share in God's
grace with me.

PHILIPPIANS 1:3, 7

4

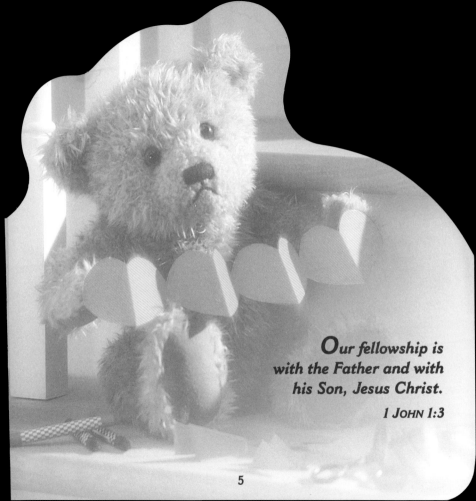

Our fellowship is
with the Father and with
his Son, Jesus Christ.

1 JOHN 1:3

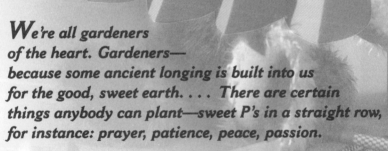

*We're all gardeners
of the heart. Gardeners—
because some ancient longing is built into us
for the good, sweet earth. . . . There are certain
things anybody can plant—sweet P's in a straight row,
for instance: prayer, patience, peace, passion.*

BARBARA JOHNSON

6

*There is a time
for everything, and a season
for every activity under heaven: . . .
God has made everything beautiful in its time.*

ECCLESIASTES 3:1,11

Jesus, where'er Thy people meet,
There they behold Thy mercy seat;
Where'er they seek Thee Thou art found,
And every place is hallowed ground.
For Thou, within no walls confined,
Dost dwell with those of humble mind;
Such ever bring Thee where they come,
And, going, take Thee to their home.

WILLIAM COWPER

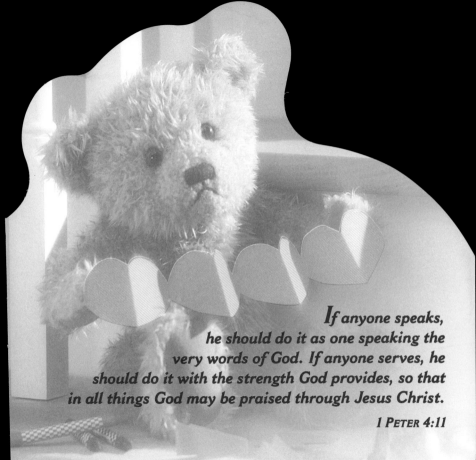

If anyone speaks,
he should do it as one speaking the
very words of God. If anyone serves, he
should do it with the strength God provides, so that
in all things God may be praised through Jesus Christ.

1 PETER 4:11

9

*Therefore my heart is glad and my tounge rejoices;
my body will also rest secure,
because you will not abandon me to the grave,
nor will you let your Holy One see decay.*

PSALM 16:9

*O*ur days are
numbered—let us spare
our anxious hearts a needless care;
'Tis Thine to number out our days,
and ours to give them to Thy praise.

JEANNE GUYON

11

All around us are friends
who seem to grow together as garden flowers.
Each one contributes a unique scent and adds a special
color to the memory of spring, summer, and fall of every
new year together.

12

So are you to my thoughts as food to life,
Or as sweet-seasoned showers are to the ground;
And for the peace of you I hold such strife
As 'twixt a miser and his wealth is found.

WILLIAM SHAKESPEARE

13

Glorify the LORD with me;
let us exalt his name together.

PSALM 34:3

*T*wo hearts that share
laughter and pain.
Two souls that share a faith.
Two minds that help each other grow.
I'm glad God made us friends.

CONOVER SWOFFORD

15

*T*wo are better than one,
 because they have a good
return for their work:
 If one falls down,
his friend can help him up.

ECCLESIASTES 4:9–10

16

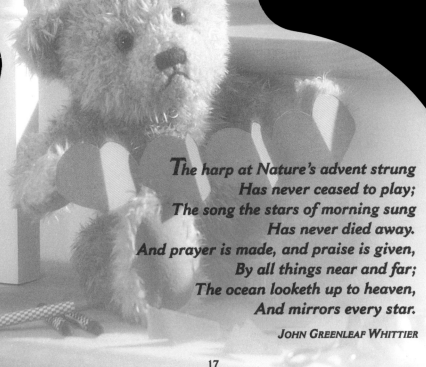

The harp at Nature's advent strung
　　Has never ceased to play;
The song the stars of morning sung
　　Has never died away.
And prayer is made, and praise is given,
　　By all things near and far;
The ocean looketh up to heaven,
　　And mirrors every star.

JOHN GREENLEAF WHITTIER

17

*G*od will meet all
your needs according to his glorious
riches in Christ Jesus.

PHILIPPIANS 4:19

18

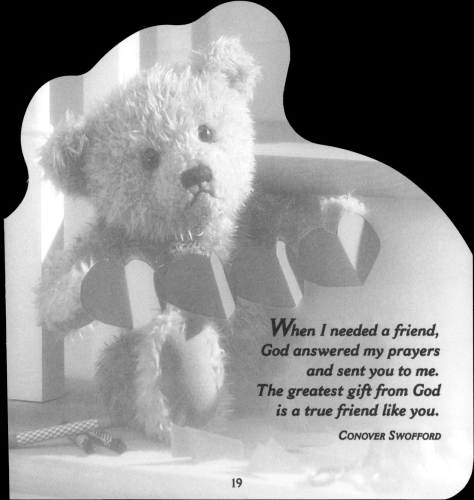

*W*hen I needed a friend,
God answered my prayers
and sent you to me.
The greatest gift from God
is a true friend like you.

CONOVER SWOFFORD

So let us, unobtrusive and unnoticed,
But happy none the less,
Be privileged to fill the air around us
With happiness;
To live, unknown beyond the cherished circle,
Which we can bless and aid;
To die, and not a heart that does not love us
Know where we're laid.

ANNIE LOUSIA WALKER

*W*hen we've been there ten thousand years,
Bright shining as the sun,
We've no less days to sing God's praise
Than when we'd first begun.

JOHN NEWTON

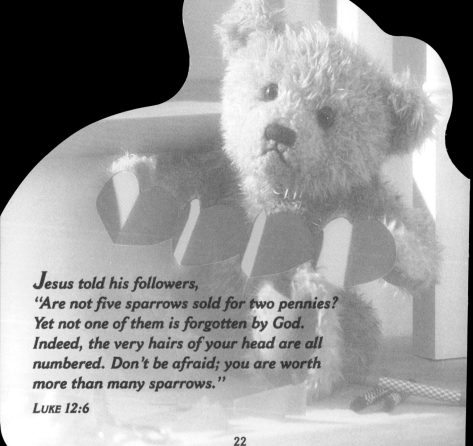

*J*esus told his followers,
"Are not five sparrows sold for two pennies?
Yet not one of them is forgotten by God.
Indeed, the very hairs of your head are all
numbered. Don't be afraid; you are worth
more than many sparrows."

LUKE 12:6

22

We always thank God,
the Father of our Lord Jesus Christ,
when we pray for you, because we have heard of your
faith in Christ Jesus and of the love you have for all
the saints the faith and love that spring from the hope that
is stored up for you in heaven and that you have already
heard about in the word of truth, the gospel.

COLOSSIANS 1:3–5

*God is love. Whoever lives
in love lives in God, and God in him.*

1 JOHN 4:17

How important one life is.
One person can make such a difference. . . .
There is something very powerful about having
someone believing in you, someone giving you
another chance. . . . If the whole purpose of our lives
is to become more like Christ, and I believe it is,
then we need real soul friendships in that process.

SHEILA WALSH

25

I like to cultivate the spirit of happiness!
It retunes my soul and keeps it perfectly in tune . . .
The chords of my soul become so vibrant and full of
heavenly electricity when my heart is full of the
happiness and joy of the Holy Spirit.

L.B. COWMAN

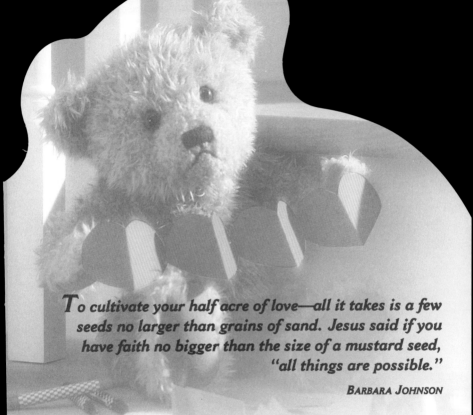

To cultivate your half acre of love—all it takes is a few seeds no larger than grains of sand. Jesus said if you have faith no bigger than the size of a mustard seed, "all things are possible."

BARBARA JOHNSON

To you, O LORD, I lift up
my soul; in you I trust, O my God. . . .
Show me your ways, O LORD, teach me your paths; guide
me in your truth and teach me, for you are God my Savior,
and my hope is in you all day long. Remember, O LORD,
your great mercy and love, for they are from of old.

PSALM 25:1–6

28

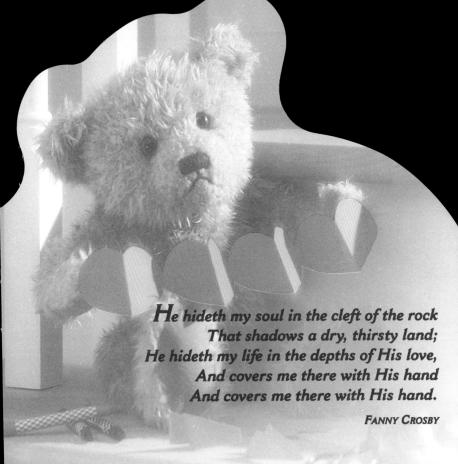

He hideth my soul in the cleft of the rock
That shadows a dry, thirsty land;
He hideth my life in the depths of His love,
And covers me there with His hand
And covers me there with His hand.

FANNY CROSBY

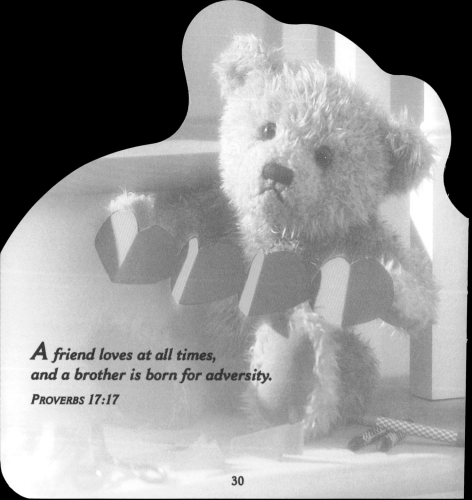

A friend loves at all times,
and a brother is born for adversity.

PROVERBS 17:17

My friend will tell me the truth
when I need to hear it. I can be confident that
she won't let me get away with too much— she'll stop me
in a loving way when I need someone to give me an honest
tug on the reins of my life.

BARBARA JOHNSON

*G*od has said,
"Never will I leave you;
never will I forsake you."
So we say with confidence,
"The Lord is my helper."

HEBREWS 13:5–6

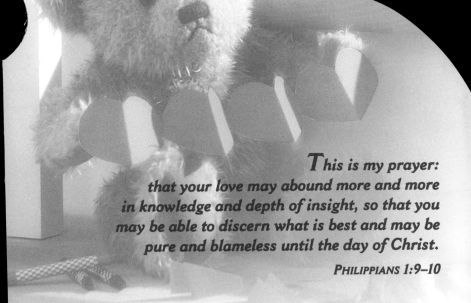

*T*his is my prayer:
that your love may abound more and more
in knowledge and depth of insight, so that you
may be able to discern what is best and may be
pure and blameless until the day of Christ.

PHILIPPIANS 1:9–10

33

I meet people whose lives flower
with the results of tiny deeds of goodness
planted year after year. The rest of us harvest
the fruit from their lives. Often they haven't got
a clue how God is using them.

BARBARA JOHNSON

Carry each other's burdens, and in this way you will fulfill the law of Christ.

GALATIANS 6:2

*Nothing but Heaven itself is
better than a friend who is really a friend.*

TITUS MACCIUS PLAUTUS

36

*Make my joy complete
by being like-minded, having the
same love, being one in spirit and purpose.*

PHILIPPIANS 2:2

*W*ounds from a friend can be trusted . . .
and the pleasantness of one's friend springs from his
earnest counsel.
Do not forsake your friend.

PROVERBS 27:5–6, 9–10

38

In all my prayers for all of you, I always pray with joy because of your partnership in the gospel from the first day until now, being confident of this, that he who began a good work in you will carry it on to completion until the day of Christ Jesus.

PHILIPPIANS 1:4–6

39

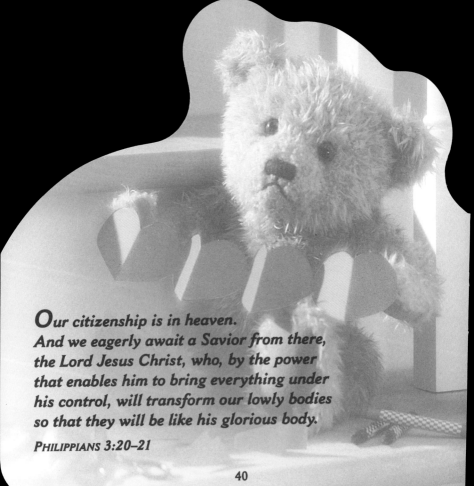

*O*ur citizenship is in heaven.
*And we eagerly await a Savior from there,
the Lord Jesus Christ, who, by the power
that enables him to bring everything under
his control, will transform our lowly bodies
so that they will be like his glorious body.*

PHILIPPIANS 3:20–21

40

Thanks be to God, who always leads us in triumphal procession in Christ and through us spreads everywhere the fragrance of the knowledge of him.

2 CORINTHIANS 2:14

*A*s we walk close to
Jesus each day, we learn to put
our confidence in Him. We learn that
the Christian life is not a series of supernatural
interventions. We become like the wise man who
build his house on the rock. When the storms came,
his house stood firm.

HOPE MACDONALD

Jesus said, "I will show you what he is like who comes to me and hears my words and puts them into practice. He is like a man building a house, who dug down deep and laid the foundation on rock. When a flood came, the torrent struck that house but could not shake it, because it was well built."

LUKE 6:47–48

43

*M*y heart leaps for joy
and *I will give thanks to the* L*ORD* *in song.*

PSALM 28:7

44

*K*eep happiness very close
to the surface of your life. . . . Open
your arms wide to God's imagination at
work in you. Be brave. Then braver still.

BARBARA JOHNSON

We have our own unique style,
Joint memories we recall;
And whenever we're together,
A good time is had by all.

CONOVER SWOFFORD

46

*The eyes of the
Lord are on the righteous
and his ears are attentive to their prayer.*

1 PETER 3:12

Be thou my vision, O Lord of my heart
Naught be all else to me, save that thou are:
Thou my best thought, by day or by night,
Waking or sleeping, thy presence my light.

ANCIENT IRISH PRAYER

TRANSLATION, MARY BYRNE

*Y*ou show that you
are a letter from Christ, . . .
written not with ink but with the
Spirit of the living God, not on tablets
of stone but on tablets of human hearts.

2 CORINTHIANS 3:3

49

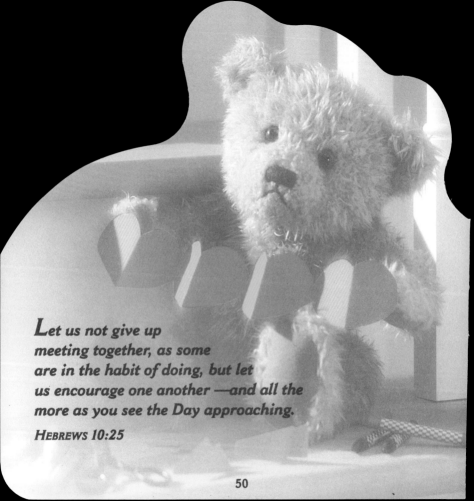

*L*et us not give up
meeting together, as some
are in the habit of doing, but let
us encourage one another —and all the
more as you see the Day approaching.

HEBREWS 10:25

I saw two children walking together today, happily exchanging words and glances, laughing aloud at shared jokes. They didn't worry about the cracks in the sidewalk or the bumps in the road, but rather skipped along over them. God wants our walk with him to be just like that—enjoying his company, sharing together.

MARGARET FISHBACK POWERS

*T*he autumn of friendship
deepens in the quiet moments only close friends
can know . . . the single word that means a whole
adventure and the loving thought that bridges any distance.
It's the time of realizing that someone will be a friend
forever and a special part of treasured memories kept
through every season of life.

PAT MITCHELL

A friend is someone
who shares with you
a smile, a tear, a hand.
A friend is someone who cares for you
a heart that can understand.
A friend is someone you can just be with,
even when there's nothing to do.
A friend is someone you can laugh with;
I'm glad my friend is you.

CONOVER SWOFFORD

53

*Jesus said,
"Love one another.
As I have loved you, so you
must love one another. By this
all men will know that you are my
disciples, if you love one another."*

JOHN 13:34–35

54

An ounce of practice is worth a pound of preaching.

AMERICAN FOLK SAYING

55

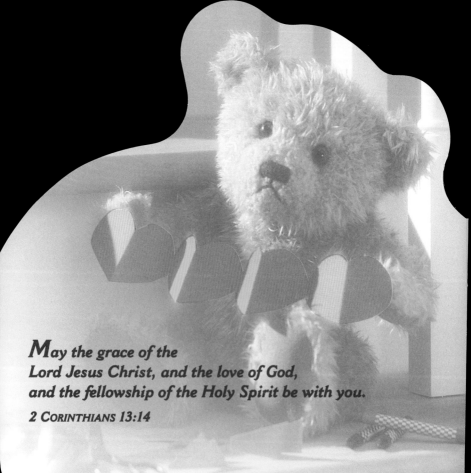

*M*ay the grace of the
Lord Jesus Christ, and the love of God,
and the fellowship of the Holy Spirit be with you.

2 CORINTHIANS 13:14

56

*Perhaps green was
God's favorite shade . . . He certainly
used a lot of it! And I love the way God and
his friends Adam and Eve could enjoy it together!
I hope God enjoys walking in my heart's garden, and
yours, as we welcome him there, having planned and
prepared it for his enjoyment.*

LUCI SHAW

*B*lessed are the peacemakers,
for they will be called sons of God.

MATTHEW 5:9

*Beauty is important to God.
He loves it. He made it. Why else would
he shape and color fish, birds, insects, plants,
and people with such astonishing diversity?*

LUCI SHAW

*Jesus is a friend with
whom you can feel safe. His friendship
is the kind George Elliot described: "Oh the comfort,
the inexpressible comfort of feeling safe with a person.
Having neither to weigh words nor measure thoughts but
pouring them all out like chaff and grain together—certain*

[continued next page]

*that a faithful hand will keep
what is worth keeping, and with a breath
of kindness, blow the rest away"* If you have a friend
like that, you have a treasure. Someone with whom you can
peel back the layers of your heart, knowing that he or she
will handle tenderly and loyally everything that's revealed.

JONI EARECKSON TADA

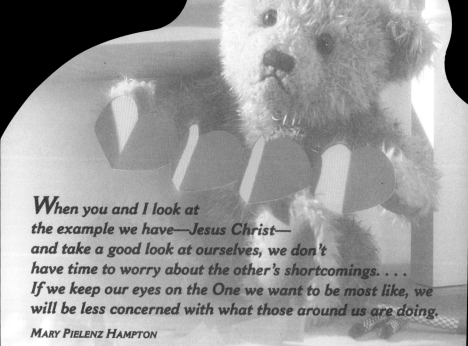

When you and I look at
the example we have—Jesus Christ—
and take a good look at ourselves, we don't
have time to worry about the other's shortcomings. . . .
If we keep our eyes on the One we want to be most like, we
will be less concerned with what those around us are doing.

MARY PIELENZ HAMPTON

62

O LORD, . . . your love
is ever before me . . . I love the
house where you live, O LORD, the place
where your glory dwells. . . . redeem me and be merciful to
me. My feet stand on level ground; in the great assembly I
will praise the LORD.

PSALM 26:2–3, 8, 11–12

One thing I ask of the LORD,
this is what I seek:
that I may dwell in the
house of the LORD
all the days of my life,
to gaze upon the beauty of the LORD. . . .
he will keep me safe in his dwelling;
he will hide me in the shelter of his tabernacle
and set me high upon a rock.

PSALM 27:4–5

*N*o matter how many promises God has made, they are "Yes" in Christ. And so through him the "Amen" is spoken by us to the glory of God. . . . It is God who makes both us and you stand firm in Christ. He anointed us, set his seal of ownership on us, and put his Spirit in our hearts as a deposit, guaranteeing what is to come.

2 CORINTHIANS 1:20–22

*N*ow to him who is able to
do immeasurably more than all we ask
or imagine, according to his power that is at work
within us, to him be glory in the church and in Christ
Jesus throughout all generations, for ever and ever! Amen.

EPHESIANS 3:20–21

*W*arm and lovely memories
have a way of helping you live life better
in the present. Think of the embrace of the friend
who led you to Jesus. Recall the time in church when
you cried as you sang a favorite hymn.... Pick out a
memory... and savor the sweetness.

JONI EARECKSON TADA

*W*hat a friend we have in Jesus,
    All our sins and griefs to bear!
What a privilege to carry
    Everything to God in prayer!

JOSEPH SCRIVEN

I have a friend who loves to take long walks with me. We talk and laugh and enjoy each other's company as we stroll along. The Lord is a lot like my friend. He enjoys walking with us as our companion on life's pathway. And he brings blessing into our lives when we walk closely with him.

MARGARET FISHBACK POWERS

69

*T*he earth can have but earth, which is his due;
My spirit is thine, the better part of me . . .
The worth of that is that which it contains,
And that is this, and this with thee remains.

WILLIAM SHAKESPEARE

70

Still upward be your onward course:
For this I pray today;
Still upward as the years go by,
And seasons pass away.

L.B. COWMAN

*How pure is the dew of the hills,
how fresh is the mountain air, how rich
the food and drink of those who dwell above, . . .
Make Him the Source, the Center, and the One.*

CHARLES HADDON SPURGEON

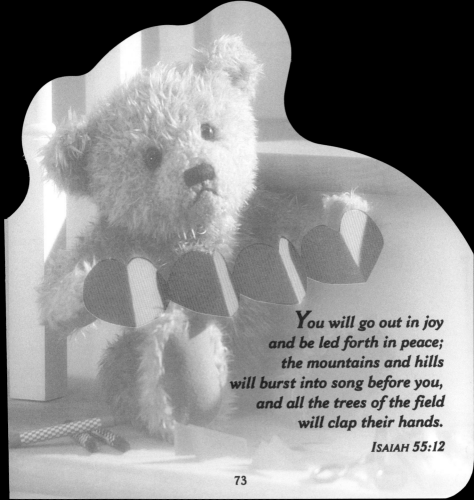

*Y*ou will go out in joy
and be led forth in peace;
the mountains and hills
will burst into song before you,
and all the trees of the field
will clap their hands.

ISAIAH 55:12

73

Some make the world a better place just by being in it.

ANONYMOUS

74

In Christ we who are many form one body, and each member belongs to all the others.

ROMANS 12:5

*Chuckles are better
than a therapist. They are aloe
vera for the sunburns of life. . . .
When the dumps take their toll, laughter
provides the exact change to get you through.*

BARBARA JOHNSON

76

A cheerful heart is good medicine.

PROVERBS 17:22

*S*hout for joy, O heavens;
rejoice, O earth;
burst into song, O mountains!
For the LORD comforts his people and will have compassion
on his afflicted ones. . . .
"See, I have engraved you on the palms of my hands;
your walls are ever before me,"
declares the LORD.

ISAIAH 49:13, 16

*T*he love of Christ places
inexorable and insistent demands on
my heart, wooing, enticing, luring, and
drawing me like a magnet. My heart is aroused
by Psalm 25:14, "the LORD confides in those who fear him."

JONI EARECKSON TADA

79

*F*ather, Thank you for the gift of friendship—
a heart to share joys and sorrows.
Thank you for this very special friend
and the love we share for each other and you.
Amen.

CONOVER SWOFFORD

Like fragrance woven through gentle breeze,
fond remembrance brings back friendship's pleasures
in every stage of life.

PAT MITCHELL

81

"*Possess your soul in patience*"
Own it, Hold your heart the way
you'd hold a live bird—in your two hands
laced to latch it in, feeling
its feathery trembling . . .
Possess it, restless, in the finger cage of patience . . .
Until morning widens like
a window, and God opens
your fingers and whispers, Fly!

LUCI SHAW

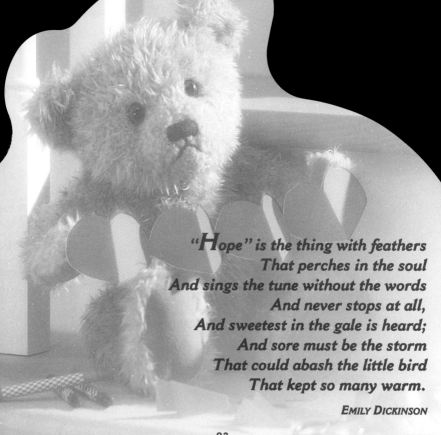

"Hope" is the thing with feathers
That perches in the soul
And sings the tune without the words
And never stops at all,
And sweetest in the gale is heard;
And sore must be the storm
That could abash the little bird
That kept so many warm.

EMILY DICKINSON

83

The charitable give out through the front door—and God gives back to them through the side window.

AMERICAN PROVERB

Hope does not disappoint us, because God has poured out his love into our hearts by the Holy Spirit, whom he has given us.

ROMANS 5:5

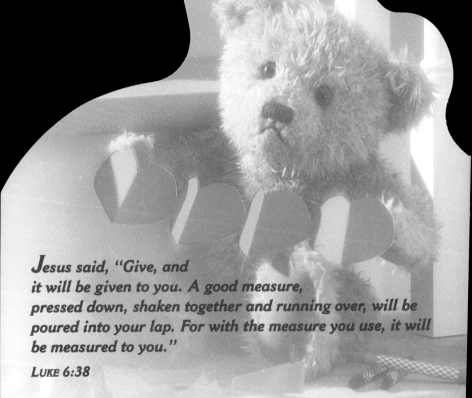

Jesus said, "Give, and
it will be given to you. A good measure,
pressed down, shaken together and running over, will be
poured into your lap. For with the measure you use, it will
be measured to you."

LUKE 6:38

Do you enjoy your friends now? You'll have more in heaven. Do you like sailing? One day you'll glide through the universe. Do you get a charge out of intellectual discussions? Soon you shall converse with the angels, the saints of the ages, and with God.

JONI EARECKSON TADA

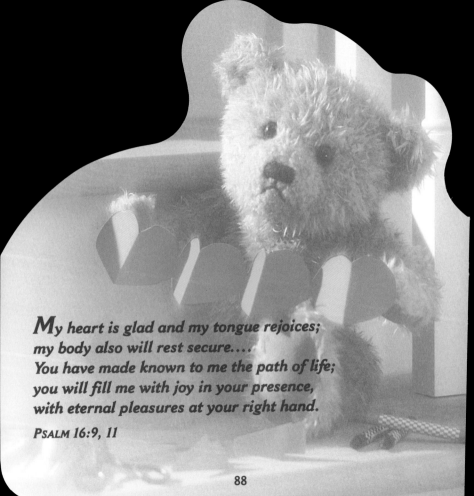

*M*y heart is glad and my tongue rejoices;
my body also will rest secure....
You have made known to me the path of life;
you will fill me with joy in your presence,
with eternal pleasures at your right hand.

PSALM 16:9, 11

88

He turned the desert into pools of water, and the parched ground into flowing springs; there he brought the hungry to live . . .

PSALM 107:35-36

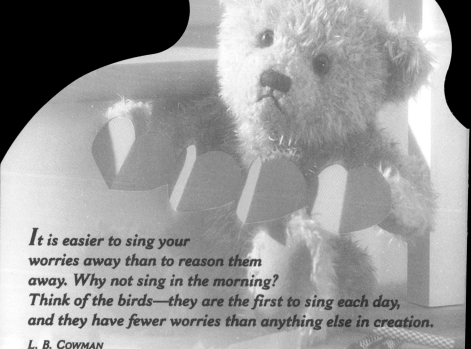

It is easier to sing your worries away than to reason them away. Why not sing in the morning? Think of the birds—they are the first to sing each day, and they have fewer worries than anything else in creation.

L. B. COWMAN

Let us hold unswervingly to the hope we profess, for he who promised is faithful.

HEBREWS 10:23

My head, my heart, mine eyes, my life, nay, more,
My joy, my magazine of earthly store,
If two be one, as surely thou and I, . . .
Wherever, ever stay, and go not thence,
Till nature's sad decree shall call thee hence;
Flesh of my flesh, bone of my bone,
I here, thou there, yet both but one.

ANNE BRADSTREET

God moves in a mysterious way,
His wonders to perform;
He plants his footsteps in the sea,
And rides upon the storm.
Deep in unfathomable mines
Of never-failing skill,
He treasures up his bright designs,
And works his sov'reign will.

WILLIAM COWPER

93

*L*ove for each other —
this is of very great importance; for
there is nothing, however annoying, that
cannot easily be borne by those who love each
other, and anything which causes annoyance must
be quite exceptional.

SAINT TERESA OF AVILA

*T*he heart has its reasons,
which reason does not know. We feel it
in a thousand things. Faith indeed tells what the senses do
not tell. It is the heart which experiences God, and not the
reason. This, then, is faith: God felt by the heart.

BLAISE PASCAL

Be devoted to one another in brotherly love.
Honor one another above yourselves.

ROMANS 12:10

*L*ove, all alike, no season knows nor clime,
Nor hours, days, months, which are the rags of time.

JOHN DONNE

97

*W*hile sorrow looks back and worry looks around,
faith looks up. You are a child of God. Take wing!

BARBARA JOHNSON

Jesus said, "Take heart!
I have overcome the world."

JOHN 16:33

Two together!
Winds blow south, or winds blow north,
Day come white, or night come black,
Home, or rivers and mountains from home,
Singing all time, minding no time,
While we two keep together.

WALT WHITMAN

100

*Rejoice in the Lord always.
I will say it again: Rejoice! Let your
gentleness be evident to all. The Lord is near. Do not be
anxious about anything, but in everything, by prayer and
petition, with thanksgiving, present your requests to God.
And the peace of God, which transcends all understanding,
will guard your hearts and your minds in Christ Jesus.*

PHILIPPIANS 4:4–7

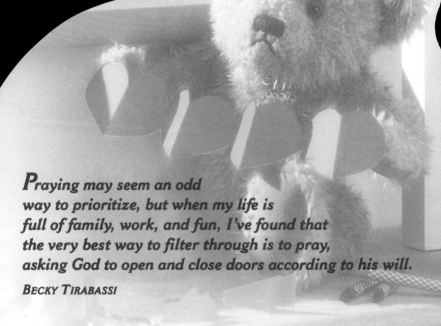

*Praying may seem an odd
way to prioritize, but when my life is
full of family, work, and fun, I've found that
the very best way to filter through is to pray,
asking God to open and close doors according to his will.*

BECKY TIRABASSI

We are richer together than when we are apart. Because of what each person brings, our lives are deepened and our vision enlarged. . . . I see in you a piece of heaven never seen before.

SHEILA WALSH

*The gift of God is
eternal life in Christ Jesus our Lord.*

ROMANS 6:23

Laughter.
The Joy of sharing the same sense of humor.
Knowledge.
Separate and shared. Yours, mine, ours.
Support.
Always there when needed to back each other up.
Friendship.
One of God's best gifts.

CONOVER SWOFFORD

Sitting under a tree on a blustery day. Pulling over on the road to take in a kaleidoscope sunset. You find yourself peeling an onion only to stop and marvel at the beauty of its concentric rings, all perfect and delicate. You see a kitten wrestling with a sock and giggle over God's sense of humor.

JONI EARECKSON TADA

*L*ove, whether newly born,
or aroused from a deathlike slumber,
must always create a sunshine, filling the heart
so full of radiance, that it overflows upon the
outward world.

NATHANIEL HAWTHORNE

Oh mighty love! Man is one world, and hath
Another to attend him.
Since then, my God, thou hast
So brave a palace built, O dwell in it,
That it may dwell with thee at last!
Till then, afford us so much wit,
That, as the world serves us, we may serve thee,
And both thy servants be.

GEORGE HERBERT

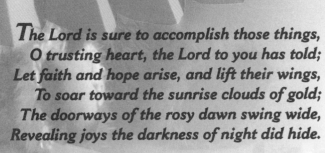

The Lord is sure to accomplish those things,
O trusting heart, the Lord to you has told;
Let faith and hope arise, and lift their wings,
To soar toward the sunrise clouds of gold;
The doorways of the rosy dawn swing wide,
Revealing joys the darkness of night did hide.

BESSIE PORTER

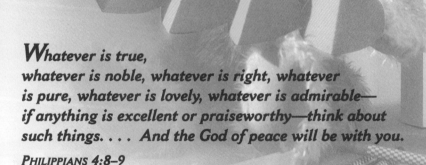

*W*hatever is true,
whatever is noble, whatever is right, whatever
is pure, whatever is lovely, whatever is admirable—
if anything is excellent or praiseworthy—think about
such things. . . . And the God of peace will be with you.

PHILIPPIANS 4:8–9

Before the hills in order stood,
Or earth receiv'd her frame,
From everlasting thou art God,
To endless years the same.
A thousand ages in thy sight
Are like an ev'ning gone;
Short as the watch that ends the night,
Before the rising sun.

ISAAC WATTS

111

Thou hidden love of God, whose height,
Whose depth unfathom'd no man knows,
I see from far thy beauteous light,
Inly I sigh for thy repose;
My heart is pain'd, nor can it be
At rest, till it finds rest in thee.

JOHN WESLEY

I will praise the LORD as long as I live,
and in your name I will lift up my hands. . . .
With singing lips my mouth will praise you.
On my bed I remember you;
I think of you through the watches of the night.

PSALM 63:4–6

Dear heavenly Father,
Help me to be one candle
lit by your love for all the world to see.
May your flame of love cause my life
to shine and bless others.
Amen.

*W*e are more than
conquerors through him
who loved us. . . . neither height
nor depth, nor anything else in all creation,
will be able to separate us from the love of God that is in
Christ Jesus our Lord.

ROMANS 8:37, 39

*K*eep a fair-sized cemetery
in your back yard, in which to bury
the faults of your friends.

HENRY WARD BEECHER

116

May God who gives encouragement give you a spirit of unity among yourselves.

ROMANS 15:5

Be like a bird that, halting in its flight,
    rests on a limb too slight.
And feeling it give way beneath him sings,
    knowing he has wings.

L. B. COWMAN

*B*ecause you are my help,
I sing in the shadow of your wings.
My soul clings to you;
your right hand upholds me.

PSALM 63:7–8

119

*N*ow you are the body
of Christ, and each one of you is a part of it.

1 CORINTHIANS 12:27

We are thankful—
even for the hard times; when we
remember we shared them with a friend and
fell into God's open arms of love through prayer.

God loves us as we are right now!
That's one of the things I'm most grateful for.
I love the freedom to be myself in God.

SHEILA WALSH

121

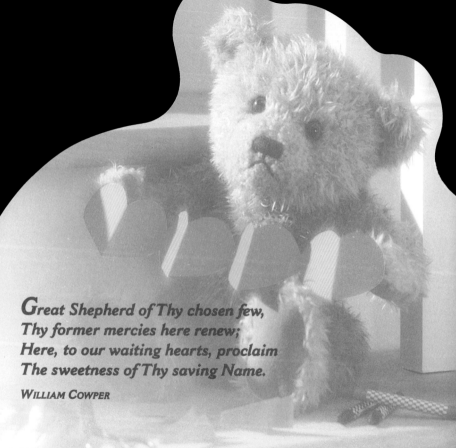

Great Shepherd of Thy chosen few,
Thy former mercies here renew;
Here, to our waiting hearts, proclaim
The sweetness of Thy saving Name.

WILLIAM COWPER

122

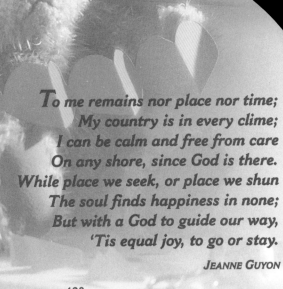

To me remains nor place nor time;
My country is in every clime;
I can be calm and free from care
On any shore, since God is there.
While place we seek, or place we shun
The soul finds happiness in none;
But with a God to guide our way,
'Tis equal joy, to go or stay.

JEANNE GUYON

123

O the pure delight of a single hour
      that before thy throne I spend,
When I kneel in prayer, and with thee, my God,
      I commune as friend with friend!
There are depths of love that I cannot know
      till I cross the narrow sea;
There are heights of joy that I may not reach
      till I rest in peace with thee.

FANNY CROSBY

Love always protects, always trusts, always hopes, always perseveres. Love never fails.

1 CORINTHIANS 13:7–8

*L*ove is patient,
love is kind. It does not envy,
it does not boast, it is not proud.
It is not rude, it is not self-seeking, it is not
easily angered, it keeps no record of wrongs.

1 CORINTHIANS 13:4–5

The LORD is my strength
and my shield; my heart trusts in him,
and I am helped.

PSALM 28:7

127

Sources

L. B. COWMAN, STREAMS IN THE DESERT, REVISED VERSION. GRAND RAPIDS: ZONDERVANPUBLISHINGHOUSE, 1997.

MARY PIELENZ HAMPTON, A TEA FOR ALL SEASONS. GRAND RAPIDS: ZONDERVANPUBLISHINGHOUSE, 1997.

BARBARA JOHNSON, BOOMERANG JOY DAYBREAK. GRAND RAPIDS: ZONDERVANPUBLISHINGHOUSE, 1998.

HOPE MACDONALD, WHEN ANGELS APPEAR. GRAND RAPIDS: ZONDERVANPUBLISHINGHOUSE, 1982.

PAT MITCHELL, LETTERS TO A DEAR FRIEND. GRAND RAPIDS: ZONDERVANPUBLISHINGHOUSE, 1997.

MARGARET FISHBACK POWERS, FOOTPRINTS: SCRIPTURE WITH REFLECTIONS INSPIRED BY THE BEST-LOVED POEM. GRAND RAPIDS: ZONDERVANPUBLISHINGHOUSE, 1998.

LUCI SHAW, WATER MY SOUL. GRAND RAPIDS: ZONDERVANPUBLISHINGHOUSE, 1998.

CONOVER SWOFFORD, YOUR FRIENDSHIP IS HEAVEN SENT. GRAND RAPIDS: ZONDERVANPUBLISHINGHOUSE, 1997.

JONI EARECKSON TADA, GOD'S PRECIOUS LOVE. GRAND RAPIDS: ZONDERVANPUBLISHINGHOUSE, 1998.

BECKY TIRABASSI, WILD THINGS HAPPEN WHEN I PRAY. GRAND RAPIDS: ZONDERVANPUBLISHINGHOUSE, 1993.

SHEILA WALSH, FAITH, HOPE, LOVE: WORDS OF INSPIRATION DAYBREAK. GRAND RAPIDS: ZONDERVANPUBLISHINGHOUSE, 1998.